LEARN TO DRAW...
UNICORNS, MERMAIDS, and MORE!

By Mara Conlon

Illustrated by Kerren Barbas Steckler

Designed by Heather Zschock

PETER PAUPER PRESS, INC.
White Plains, New York

For Copeland, Emily, and Audrey

PETER PAUPER PRESS

In 1928, at the age of twenty-two, Peter Beilenson began printing books on a small press in the basement of his parents' home in Larchmont, New York. Peter—and later, his wife, Edna—sought to create fine books that sold at "prices even a pauper could afford."

Today, still family owned and operated, Peter Pauper Press continues to honor our founders' legacy of quality, value, and fun for big kids and small kids alike.

Illustrations copyright © 2019 Kerren Barbas Steckler
Designed by Heather Zschock

Copyright © 2019
Peter Pauper Press, Inc.
Manufactured for Peter Pauper Press, Inc.
202 Mamaroneck Avenue
White Plains, NY 10601 USA
All rights reserved
ISBN 978-1-4413-3115-1
Printed in China

Published in the United Kingdom and Europe by
Peter Pauper Press, Inc. c/o White Pebble International
Unit 2, Plot 11 Terminus Road
Chichester, West Sussex PO19 8TX, UK

7 6 5 4 3 2 1

Hey, young artists!

Are you ready to learn how to draw 39 different unicorns, mermaids, and other magical things? It's easy and fun! Just follow these steps:

· ·

First, pick a unicorn, mermaid, or other picture you want to draw.

Next, trace over the picture with a pencil. This will give you a feel for how to draw the lines.

Then, following the numbers, start drawing each new step **(shown in red)** of the picture in the empty space in each scene, or on a piece of paper.

Lastly, if you're an awesome artist (and of course, you are!), try drawing a whole scene with one or more unicorns and mermaids. And remember, don't worry if your drawings look different from the ones in this book—no two unicorns or mermaids are exactly alike!

You're on your way to creating your own special masterpieces!

GET READY! GET SET! DRAW!

1.

To begin: Lightly draw these basic shapes.

2.

Then: Follow each new step in red to draw this unicorn.

3.

4.

5.

6.

7.

8.

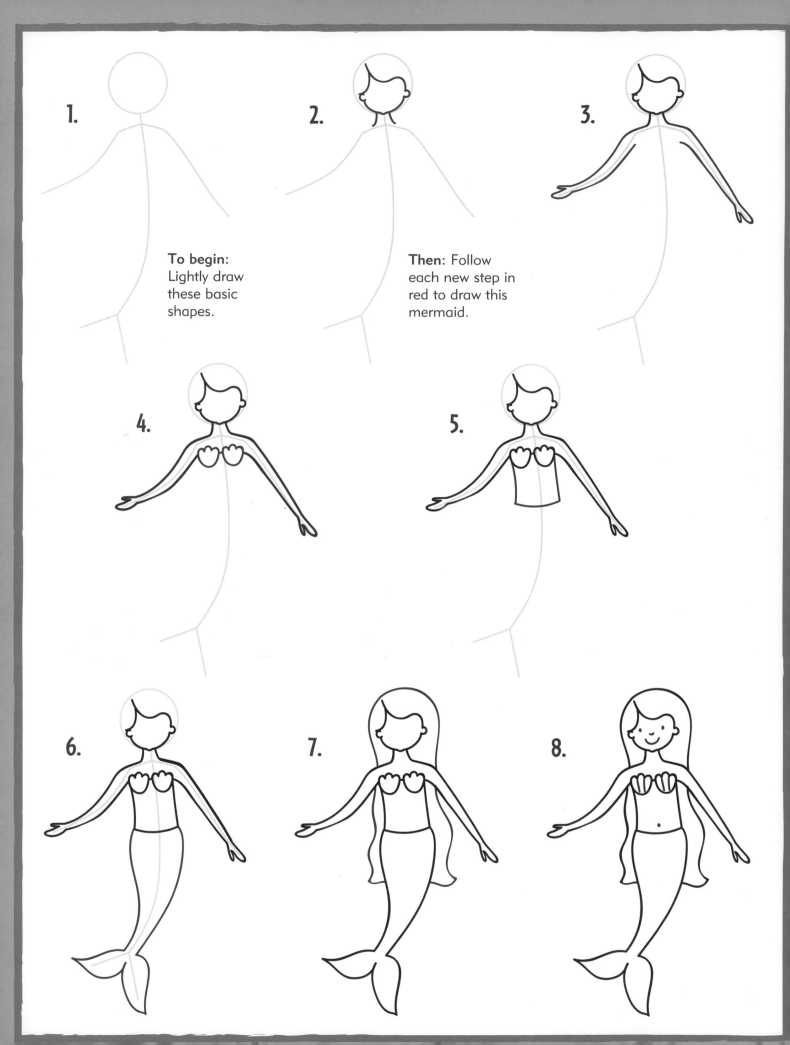

1.

To begin:
Lightly draw
these basic
shapes.

2.

Then: Follow
each new step in
red to draw this
mermaid.

3.

4.

5.

6.

7.

8.

1.

2.
Then: Follow each new step in red to draw this lightning bolt.

To begin: Lightly draw these basic shapes.

3.

1.

2.

3.

4.

1.

2.

3.

1.

2.

3.
believe

Trace over us for practice!

believe

believe

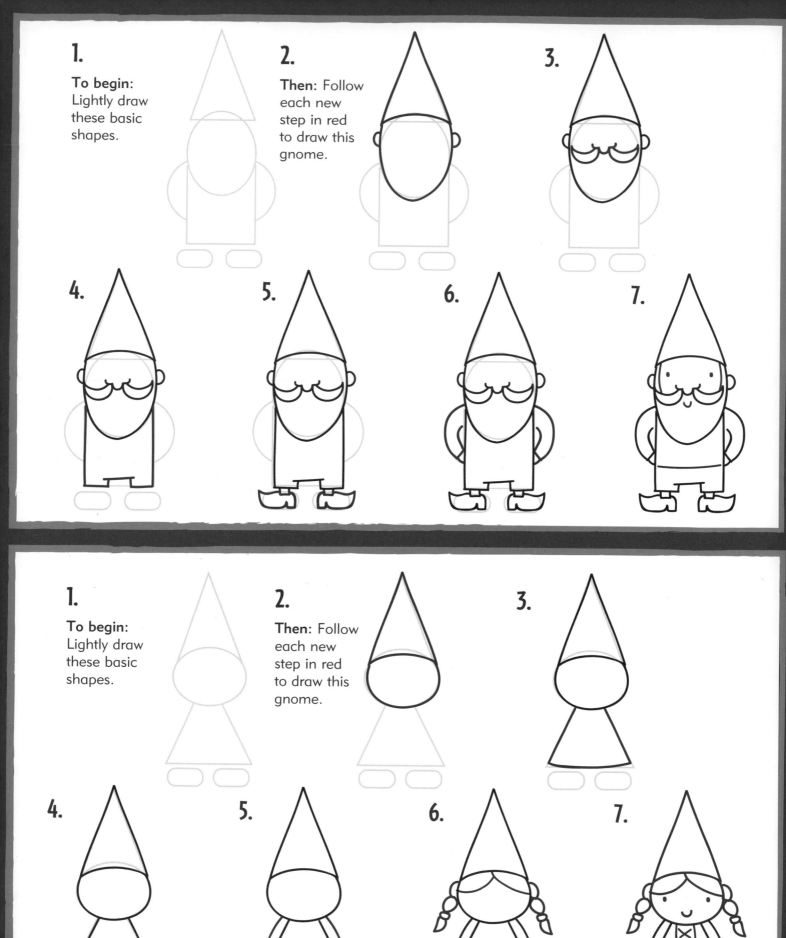

1.

To begin: Lightly draw these basic shapes.

2.

Then: Follow each new step in red to draw this gnome.

3.

4.

5.

6.

7.

1.

To begin: Lightly draw these basic shapes.

2.

Then: Follow each new step in red to draw this gnome.

3.

4.

5.

6.

7.

1.

To begin: Lightly draw these basic shapes.

2.

Then: Follow each new step in red to draw this unicorn.

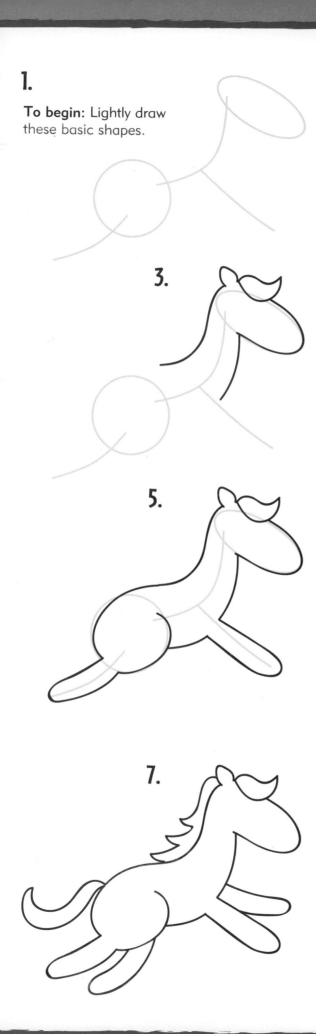
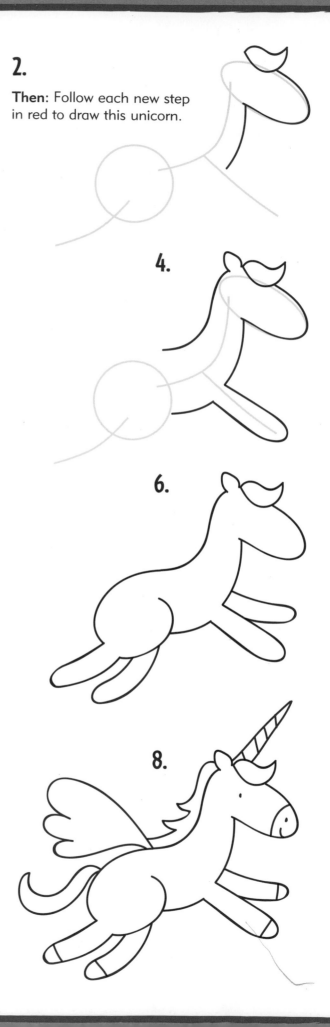

3.

4.

5.

6.

7.

8.

1.

To begin: Lightly draw these basic shapes.

2.

Then: Follow each new step in red to draw this clamshell.

3.

4.

5.

6.

1.

To begin: Lightly draw these basic shapes.

2.

Then: Follow each new step in red to draw this narwhal.

3.

4.

5.

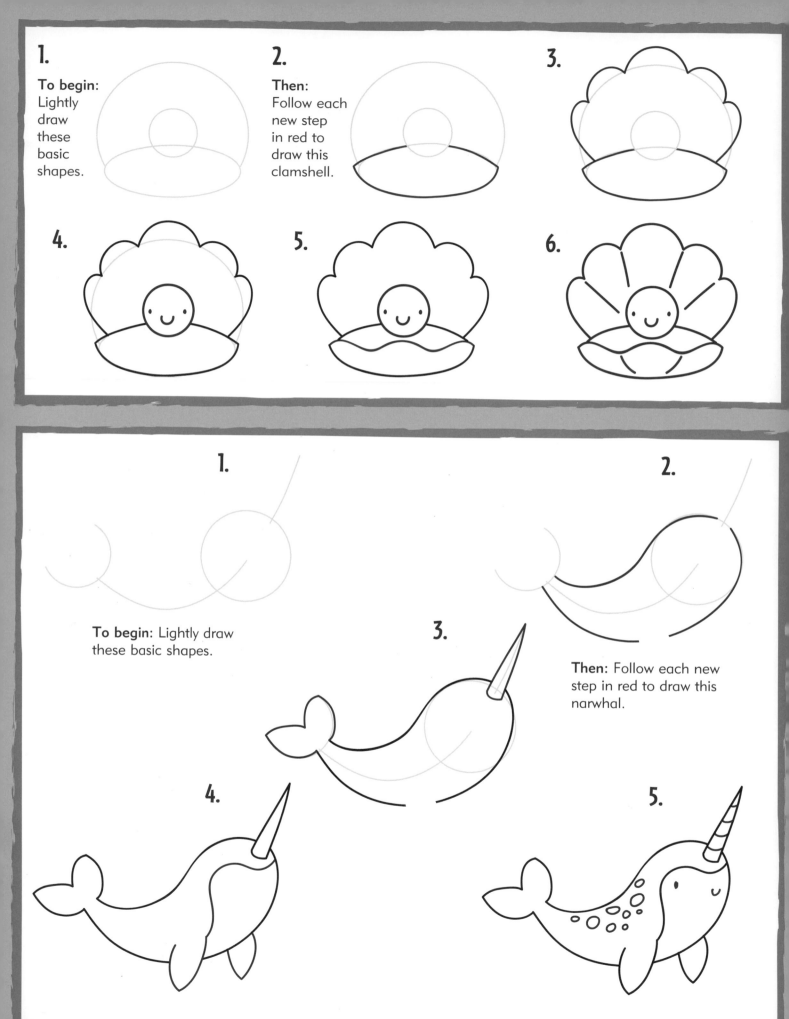

Trace over us for practice!

1.

2.

3.

4.

1.

2.

3.

4.

1.

2.

3.

5.

4.

2.

3.

4.

1.

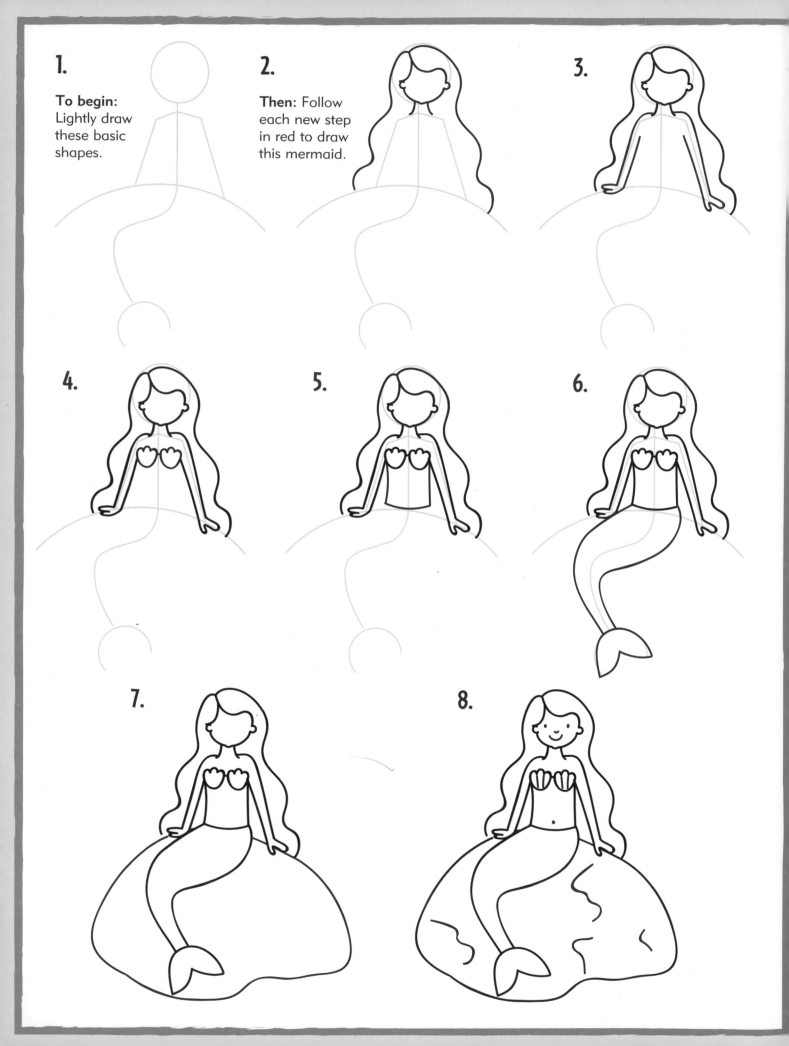

1.

To begin: Lightly draw these basic shapes.

2.

Then: Follow each new step in red to draw this mermaid.

3.

4.

5.

6.

7.

8.

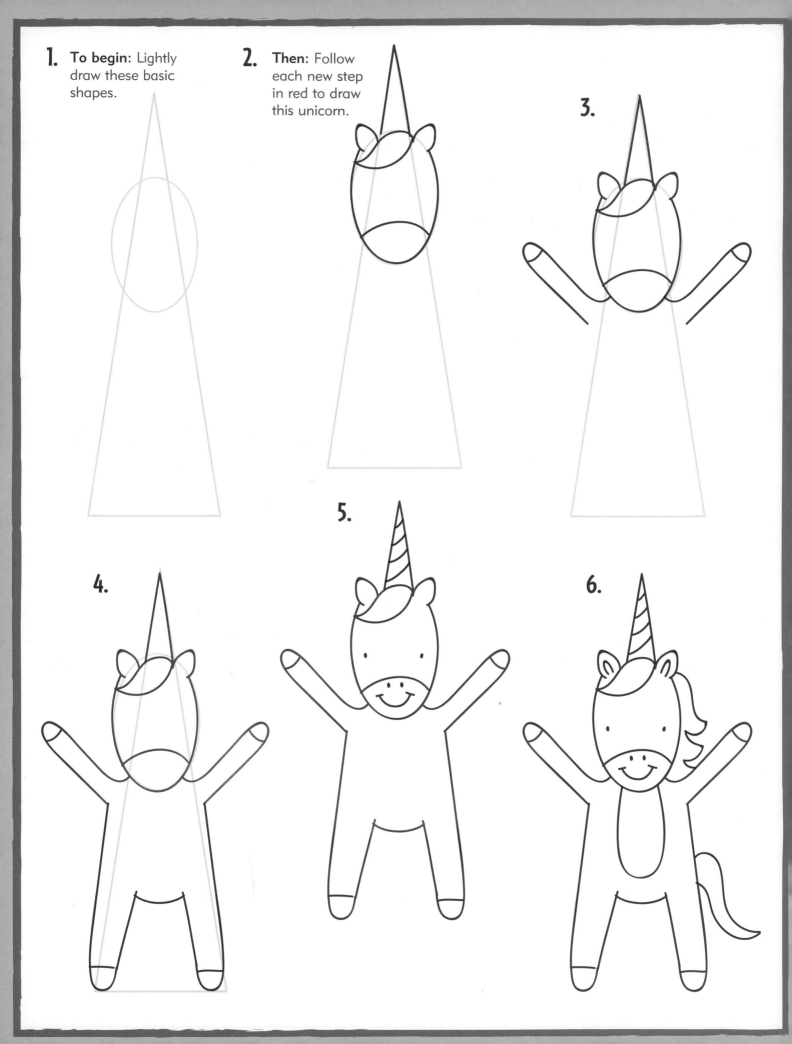

1. **To begin:** Lightly draw these basic shapes.

2. **Then:** Follow each new step in red to draw this unicorn.

3.

4.

5.

6.

To begin: Lightly draw these basic shapes.

Then: Follow each new step in red to draw this popsicle.

1.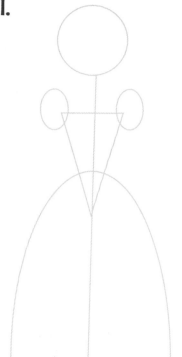

2.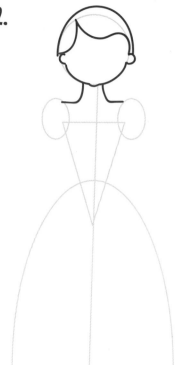

3.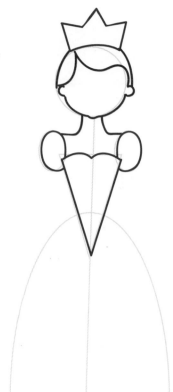

To begin: Lightly draw these basic shapes.

Then: Follow each new step in red to draw this princess.

4.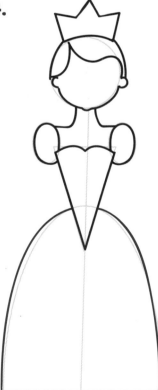

5.

6.

1.

2.

1.

To begin: Lightly draw these basic shapes.

2.

Then: Follow each new step in red to draw this tree.

3.

4.

1.

To begin: Lightly draw these basic shapes.

2.

Then: Follow each new step in red to draw this castle.

3.

4.

5.

6.

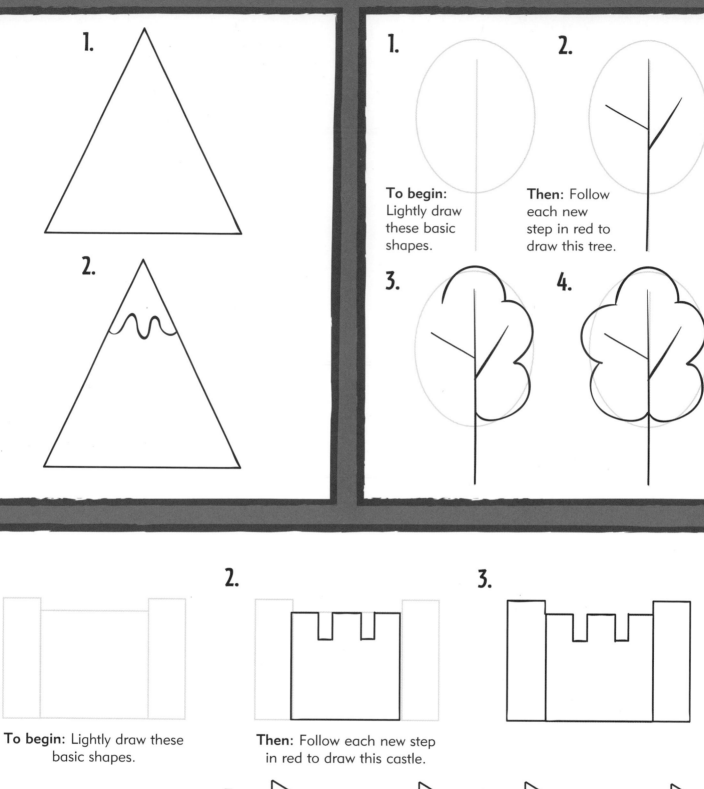

1. **To begin:** Lightly draw these basic shapes.

2. **Then:** Follow each new step in red to draw this unicorn.

3.

4.

5.

6.

7.

8.

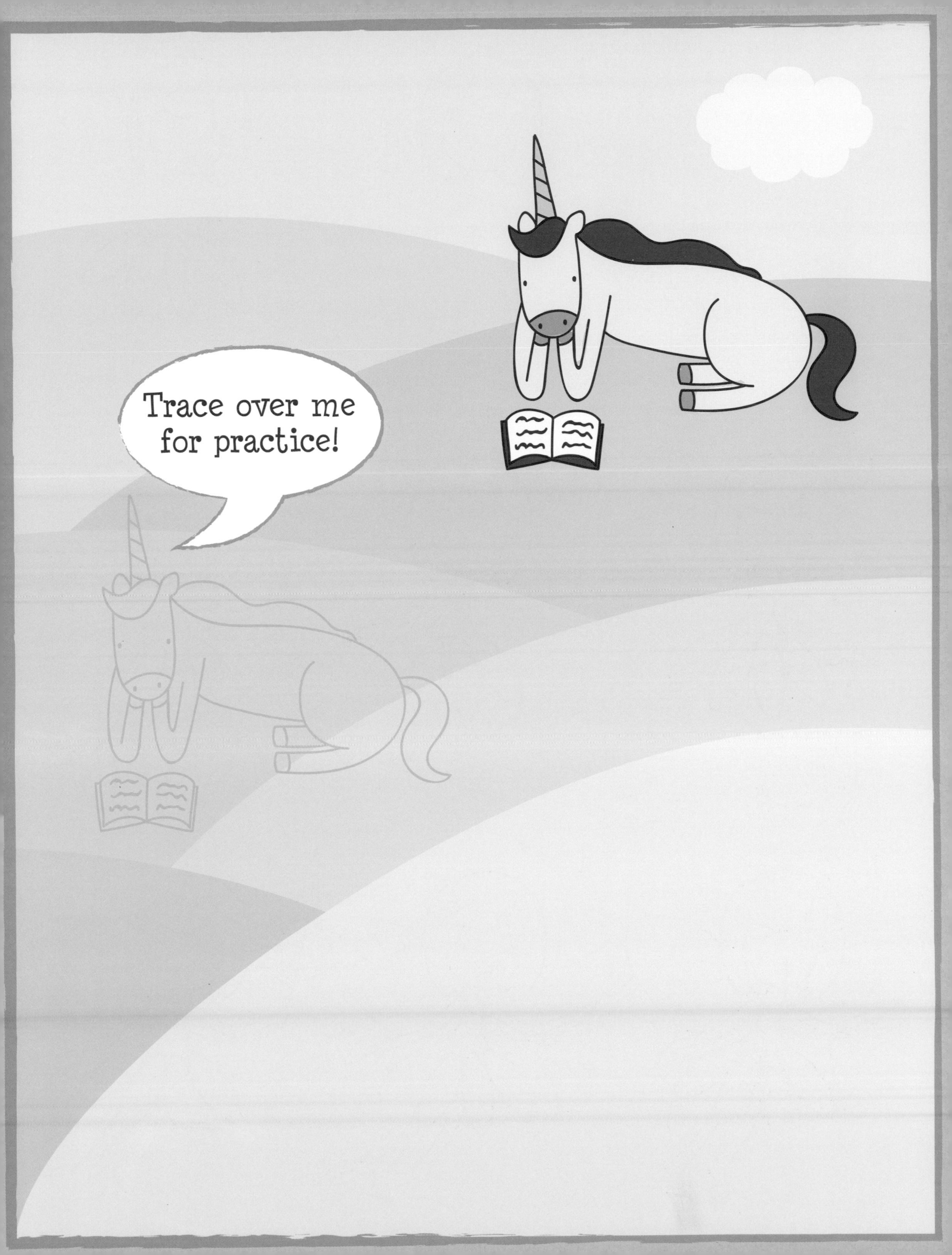
Trace over me for practice!

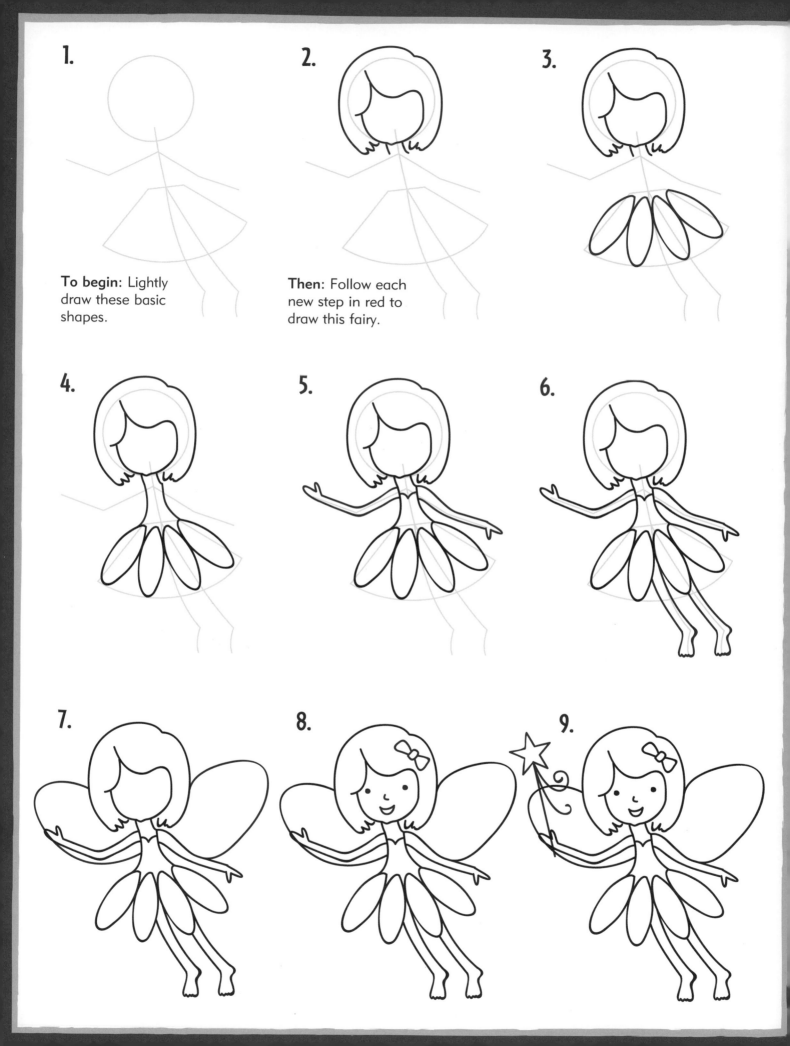

1.

To begin: Lightly draw these basic shapes.

2.

Then: Follow each new step in red to draw this fairy.

3.

4.

5.

6.

7.

8.

9.

Trace over me for practice!

1.

2.

3.

4.

5.

6.

1.

2.

To begin: Lightly draw this basic shape.

Then: Follow each new step in red to draw this flower.

3.

4.

1.

2.

3.

4.

1.

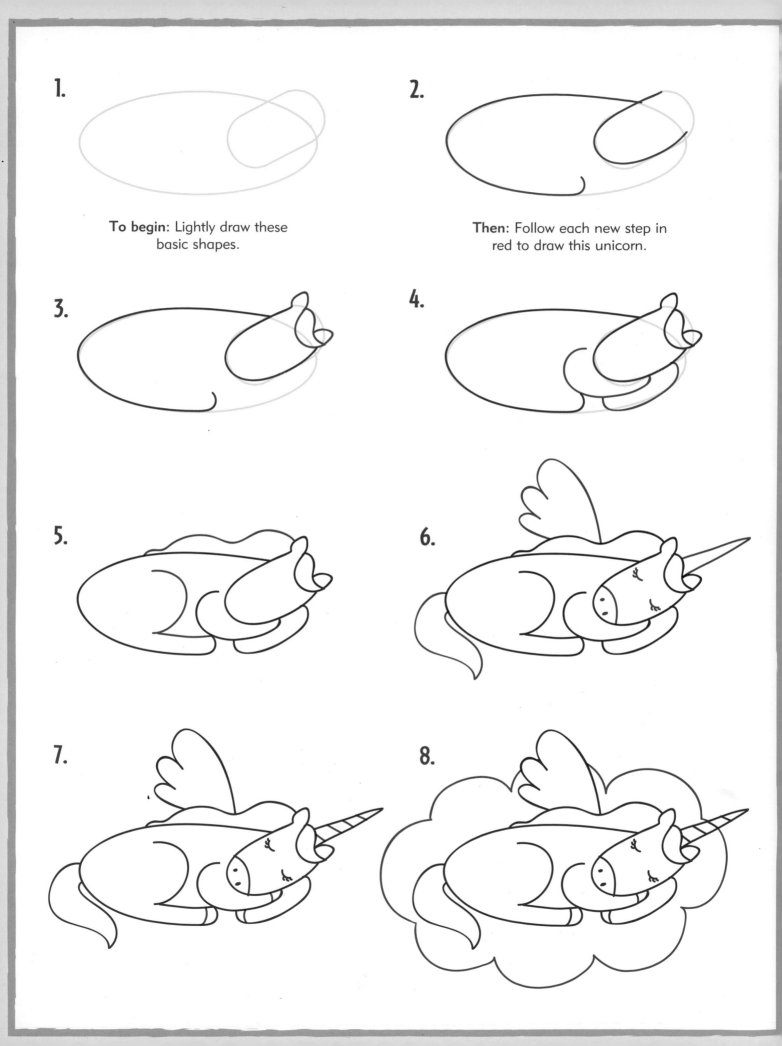

To begin: Lightly draw these basic shapes.

2.

Then: Follow each new step in red to draw this unicorn.

3.

4.

5.

6.

7.

8.

Trace over me
for practice!

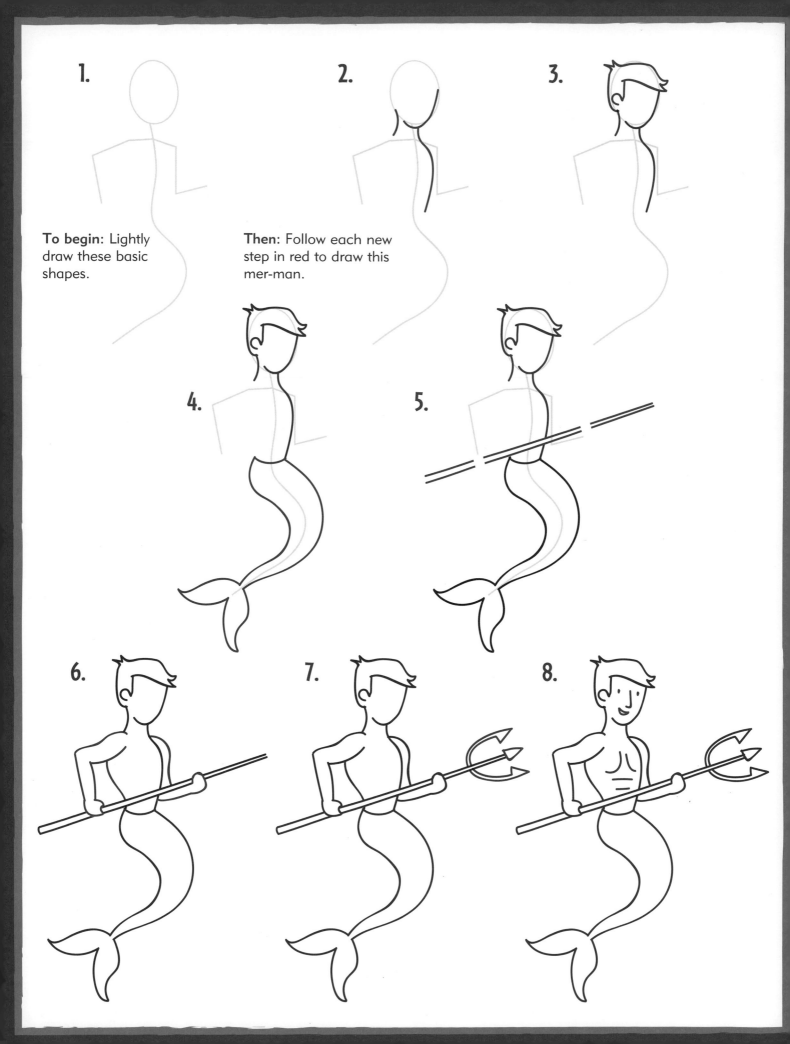

1.

To begin: Lightly draw these basic shapes.

2.

Then: Follow each new step in red to draw this mer-man.

3.

4.

5.

6.

7.

8.

1.

To begin: Lightly draw these basic shapes.

2.

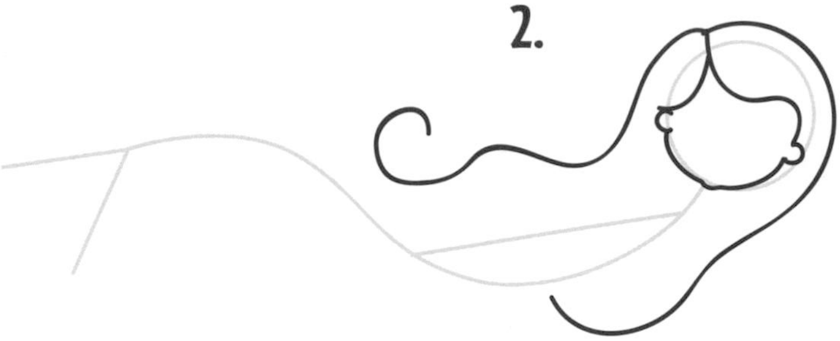

Then: Follow each new step in red to draw this mermaid.

3.

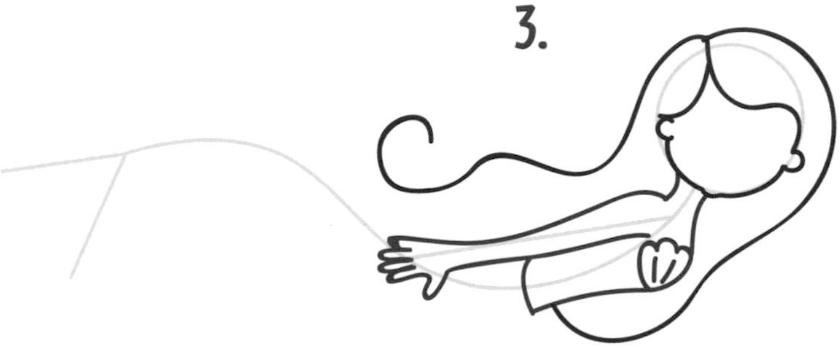

4.

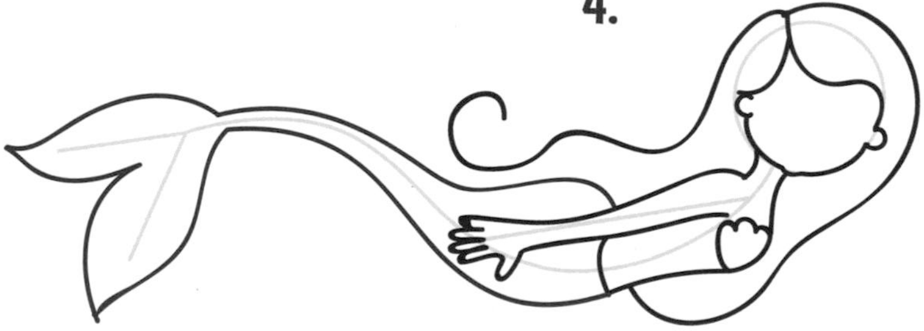

5.

6.

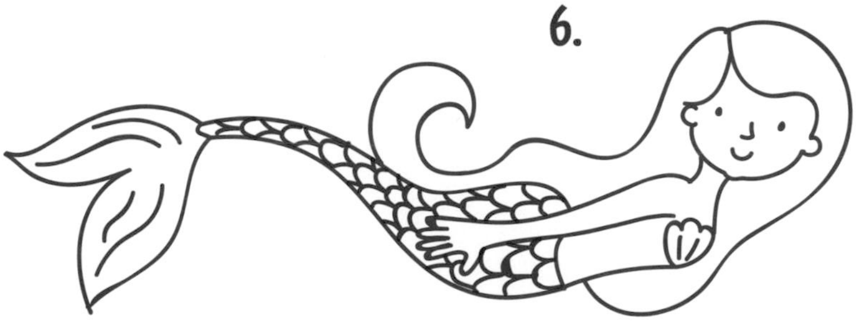

1.

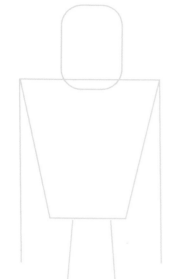

To begin: Lightly draw these basic shapes.

2.

Then: Follow each new step in red to draw this knight.

3.

4.

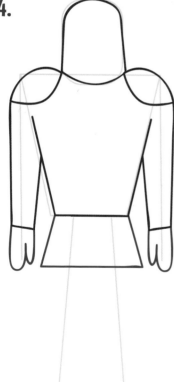

5.

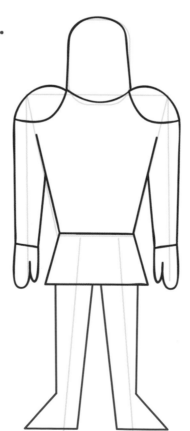

6.

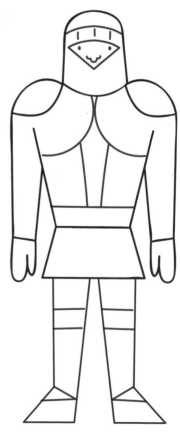

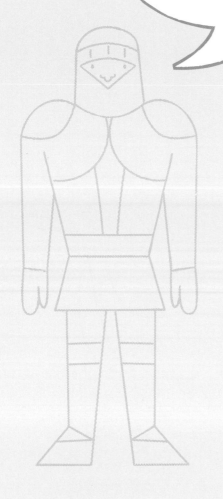

Trace over me for practice!

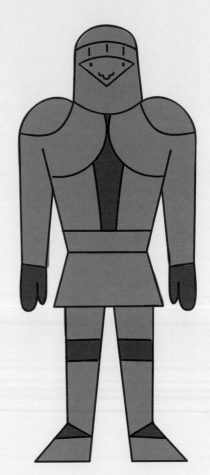

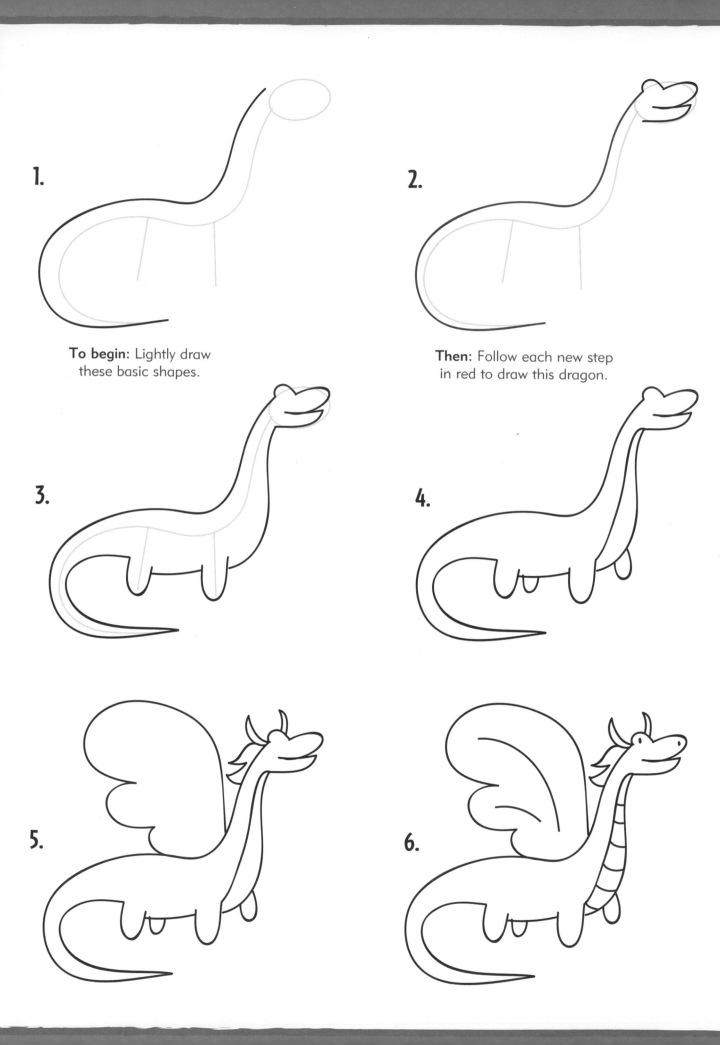

1.

To begin: Lightly draw these basic shapes.

2.

Then: Follow each new step in red to draw this dragon.

3.

4.

5.

6.

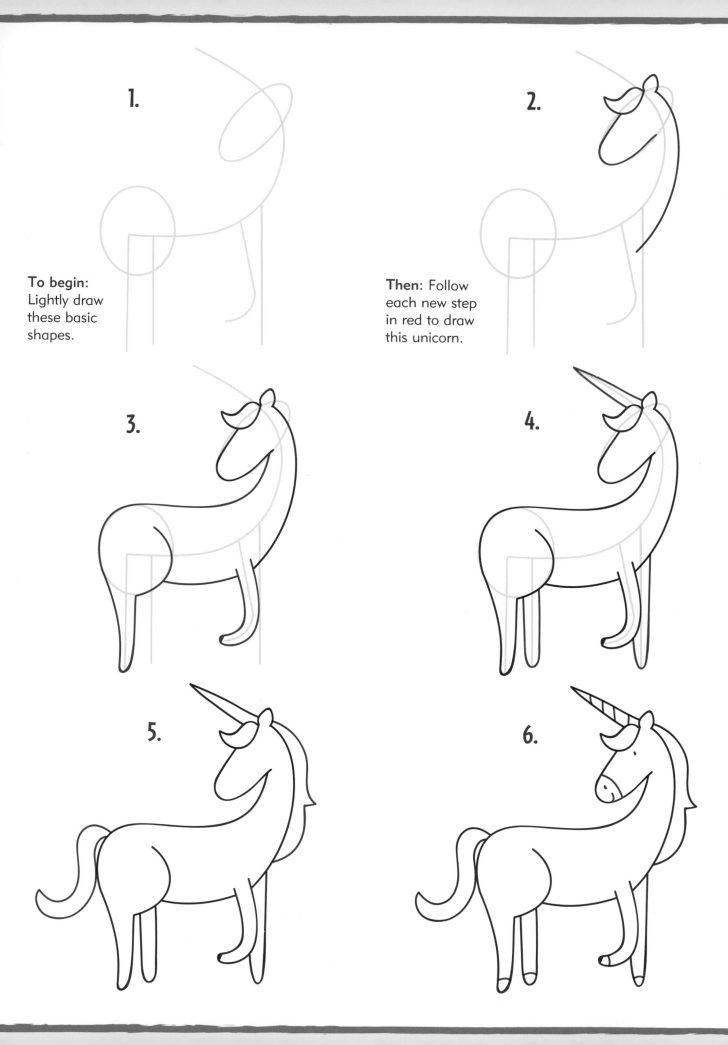

1.

To begin: Lightly draw these basic shapes.

2.

Then: Follow each new step in red to draw this unicorn.

3.

4.

5.

6.

Trace over me for practice!

We've reached the end,
and now we're done.

Drawing unicorns
and friends is
so much fun!